SPAIN

WORLD ADVENTURES
BY STEFFI CAVELL-CLARKE

KidHaven
PUBLISHING

Published in 2019 by
KidHaven Publishing, an Imprint of Greenhaven Publishing, LLC
353 3rd Avenue, Suite 255, New York, NY 10010

© 2019 Booklife Publishing

This edition is published by arrangement with Booklife Publishing.

Designer: Natalie Carr
Writer: Steffi Cavell-Clarke

Cataloging-in-Publication Data

Names: Cavell-Clarke, Steffi.
Title: Spain / Steffi Cavell-Clarke.
Description: New York : KidHaven Publishing, 2019. | Series: World adventures | Includes index.
Identifiers: ISBN 9781534526242 (pbk.) | 9781534526235 (library bound) | ISBN 9781534526259 (6 pack) | ISBN 9781534526266 (ebook)
Subjects: LCSH: Spain–Juvenile literature.
Classification: LCC DP17.C38 2019 | DDC 946–dc23

Printed in the United States of America

CPSIA compliance information: Batch # BS18KL: For further information contact Greenhaven Publishing LLC, New York, New York at 1-844-317-7404.

CONTENTS

Words in **bold** can be found in the glossary on page 24.

WHERE IS SPAIN?

SPAIN

SPAIN

Spain is a country in southwest Europe. The capital city of Spain is called Madrid.

BARCELONA

The **population** of Spain is over 46 million. Most people in Spain live in the big cities, such as Madrid and Barcelona.

WEATHER AND LANDSCAPE

Spain has a fairly warm **climate**. In the summer, Spain is usually very warm and sunny.

Spain has long stretches of beaches and high mountains. Lots of **tourists** visit Spain for the sunny weather and to spend time on the beaches.

CLOTHING

People in Spain mostly wear comfortable and **modern** clothing because of the warm climate.

8

At **festivals**, Spanish people often wear **traditional** clothing. Women dancers wear long dresses in bright colors.

FLAMENCO DANCER

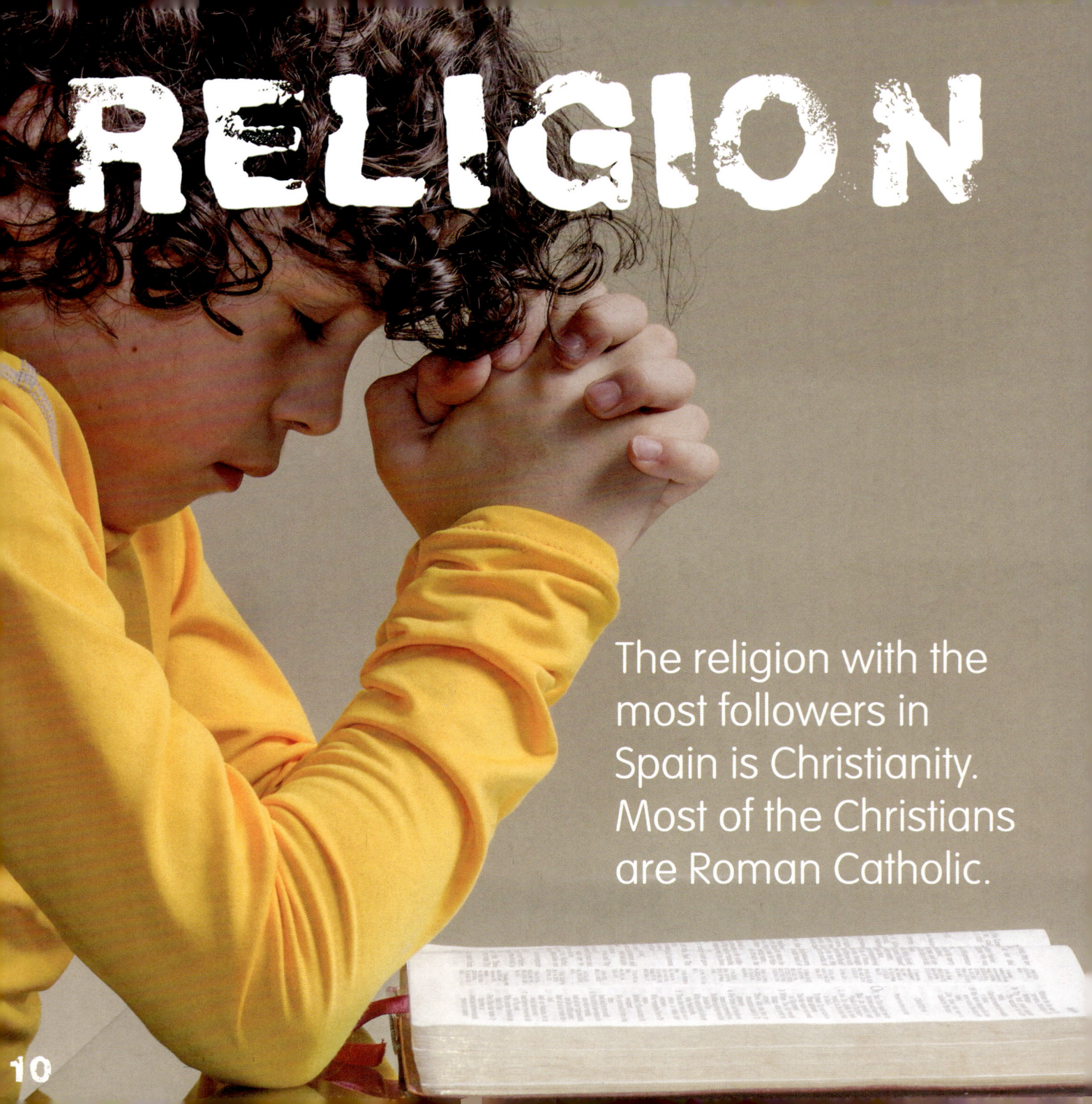

RELIGION

The religion with the most followers in Spain is Christianity. Most of the Christians are Roman Catholic.

The Roman Catholic place of **worship** is a church. People visit the church every Sunday for prayer.

SAGRADA FAMILIA

11

FOOD

PAELLA

One of the traditional meals in Spain is called paella. It is a spicy rice dish that can have meat, fish, and vegetables in it.

Tapas is also very popular in Spain. Tapas is a group of small bowls of tasty food, such as olives and seafood and special breads.

AT SCHOOL

Children in Spain start school at the age of six. They study lots of subjects, such as Spanish, science, geography, and math.

Some children also go to after-school clubs, where they can play games and sports. Lots of children love to play soccer.

AT HOME

In towns and cities, many people in Spain live in modern apartments.

MODERN APARTMENTS IN BARCELONA

There are also lots of farms in Spain. Farmers grow lots of crops, such as oranges, lemons, and olives.

FAMILIES

Most children live with their parents and **siblings**. Parents tend to go to work while the children go to school.

Spanish families like to get together for special occasions, such as weddings and religious holidays.

SPORTS

REAL MADRID SOCCER TEAM

Soccer is the most popular sport in Spain. The top soccer teams in the country are Real Madrid and FC Barcelona.

Other sports, such as tennis and basketball, are also very popular in Spain.

FUN FACTS

Spain has its own royal family. They live in a large palace outside the city of Madrid.

ROYAL PALACE OF MADRID

The flamenco is a Spanish dance. People dance the flamenco on special occasions.

GLOSSARY

climate: the weather in a large area

festivals: special occasions that are celebrated

modern: something that has been made using recent ideas

population: amount of people living in that place

siblings: brothers and sisters

tourists: visitors from other countries

traditional: ways of behaving that have been done for a long time

worship: a religious act such as praying

INDEX